SECOND EDITION

Workbook

0

Herbert Puchta · Peter Lewis-Jones

CAMBRIDGE
UNIVERSITY PRESS

Contents

Say Hello!

1 🎧 01 **Listen and say the names. Colour.**

1 **Match and say.**

1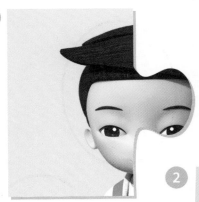

a

2

b

2 🎧 02 **Listen and match.**

1  Listen and colour.

2 Match and say.

1 2 3 4 5 6

1 🎧 04 **Listen and point. Say the numbers.**

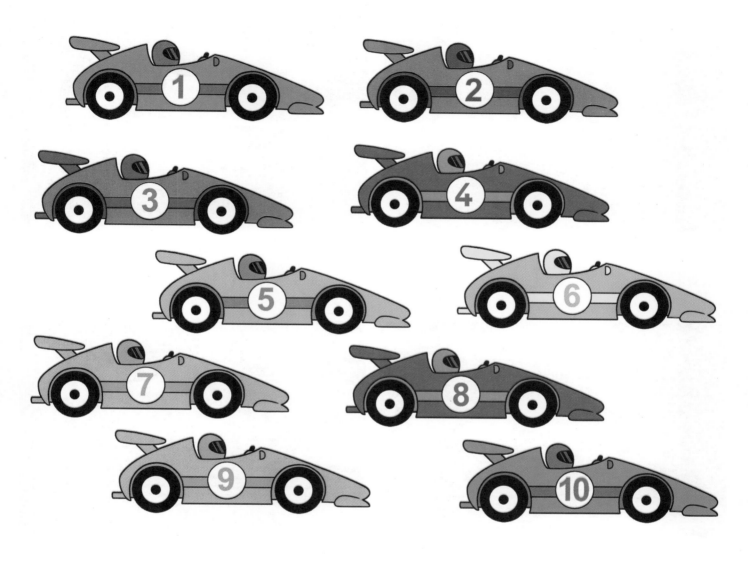

2 **Point and say. Count.**

1, 2, 3

1 🎧 05 **Listen and match.**

2 🎧 06 **Listen and point.**

1  What's good? Draw 😊.

2 Complete the picture. Draw yourself making friends.

1 My classroom

1 🎧 07 **Listen and match. Say.**

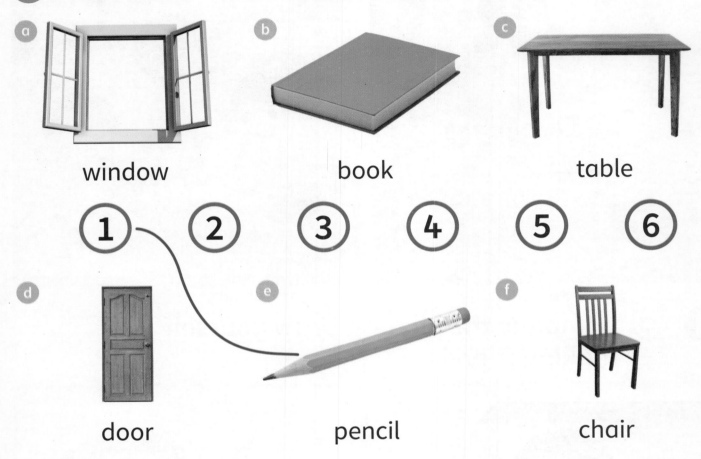

a — window
b — book
c — table

① ② ③ ④ ⑤ ⑥

d — door
e — pencil
f — chair

2 🎧 08 **Listen and colour.**

1 🎧 09 Listen and colour.

2 🎧 10 Listen. Point and say.

sit down

1 🎧 11 Listen. Point and sing.

2 🛡 Draw yourself in your classroom. Point and say.

1 🎧 12 Listen and circle.

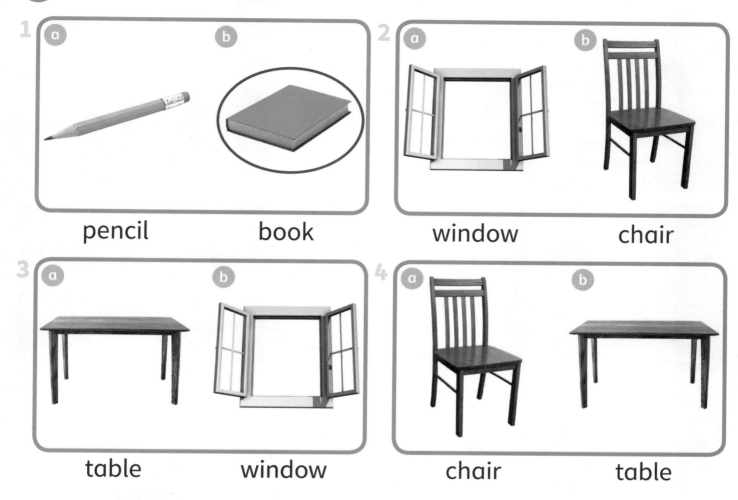

1 a b
pencil   book

2 a b
window   chair

3 a b
table   window

4 a b
chair   table

2 🎧 13 Listen and point. Say.

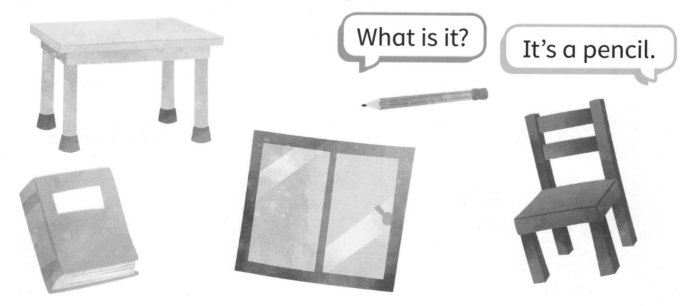

What is it?

It's a pencil.

1 🎧14 Listen and match.

a

b

c

1

2

3

4

d

2 Look and match.

1

a

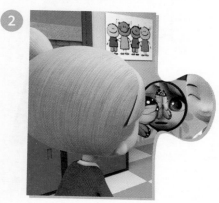

2

b

1 🛡 **What's good? Draw** 😊 **.**

2 🛡 **Look and find your favourite picture. Draw** 😊 **.**

My favourite is …

1 🎧 15 **Listen and colour.**

2 **Point and say the numbers.**

| 1 | ? | 3 | ? | 5 | ? | 7 | ? | 9 | ? |

3 🛡 **Look and say what's next.**

4 🛡 Find the wrong picture. Cross it out.

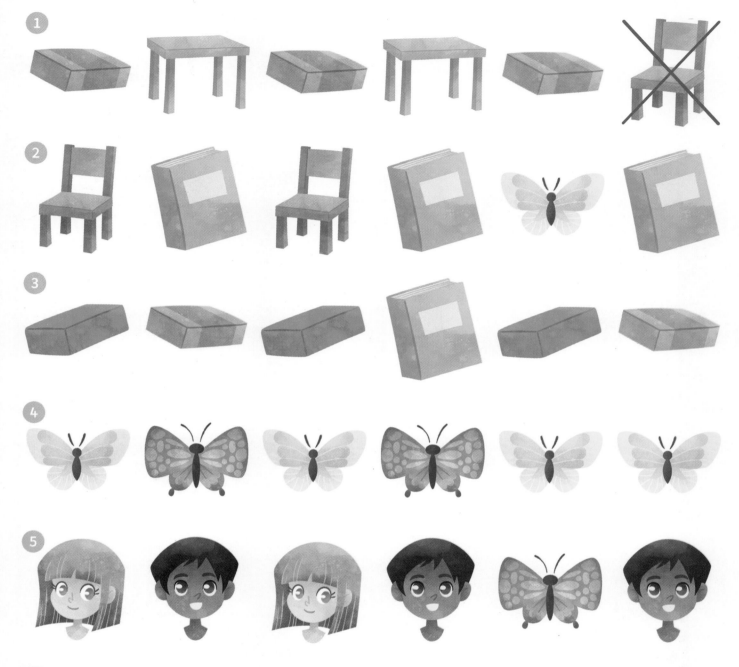

5 Complete the pattern. Say.

1 🎧 16 Where does the butterfly go? Listen and draw.

1 Look and say. Circle 😊, 😐 or 😔.

1

2

3

4

2 What's in your classroom? Circle ✓ or ✗.

BIG QUESTION What's in my classroom?

1  ✓ ✗

2 ✓ ✗

3  ✓ ✗

4  ✓ ✗

3 Colour the objects.

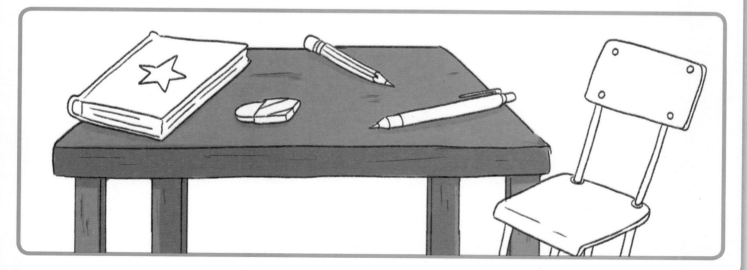

2 My body

1 🎧 17 **Listen and match. Say.**

2 🎧 18 **Listen and colour.**

1 🎧 19 **Listen to the monsters. Match.**

① ② ③ ④

a b c d

2 🛡 **Point. What does the monster say?**

I've got 2 noses.

I've got ...

1   **Listen. Trace and colour.**

2 **Look and match. Colour.**

1 🎧 21 **Listen to the monster. Circle ☑ or ☒.**

1. ☑ (☒)
2. ☑ ☒
3. ☑ ☒
4. ☑ ☒
5. ☑ ☒
6. ☑ ☒

2 **Look and remember. Cover. Ask and answer.**

What is it?

It's a nose!

1 🎧22 Listen and match.

a

b

c

① ② ③

2 🎧23 Listen and circle.

5

a

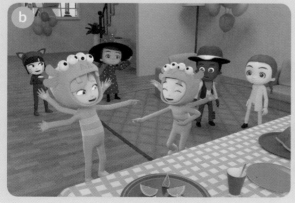
b

6

a

b

1 What's good? Draw 😊.

2 Look and circle 😊 or 😣.

1 🎧 24 Listen and match. Say.

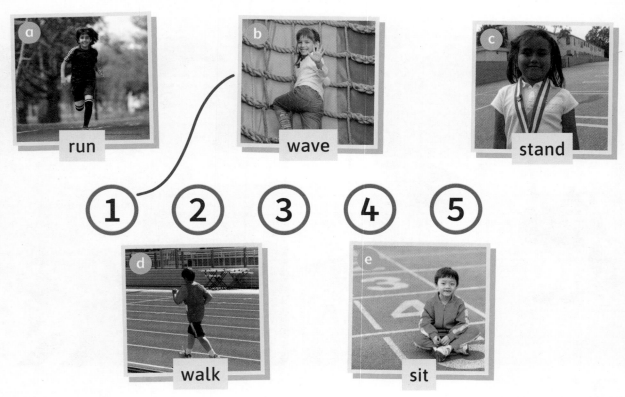

a — run
b — wave
c — stand
d — walk
e — sit

1 2 3 4 5

2 🎧 25 Listen and circle ☑ or ☒.

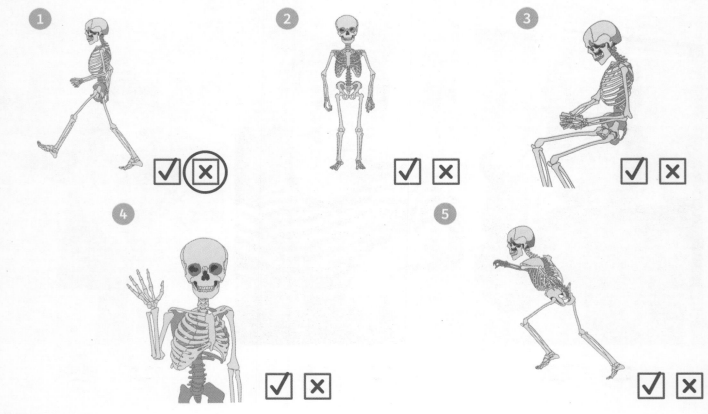

1 ☑ ⊗
2 ☑ ☒
3 ☑ ☒
4 ☑ ☒
5 ☑ ☒

3 🎧26 **Listen and colour.**

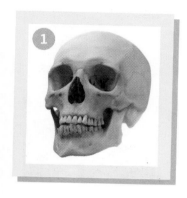

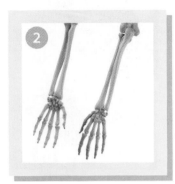

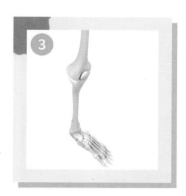

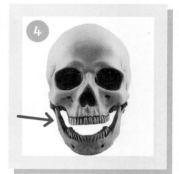

4 🎧27 **Listen and match.**

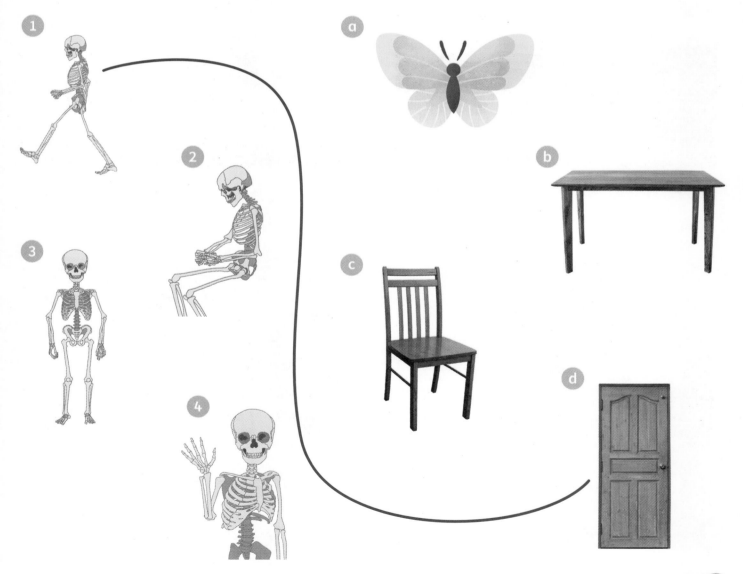

1 🎧 28 Listen and colour.

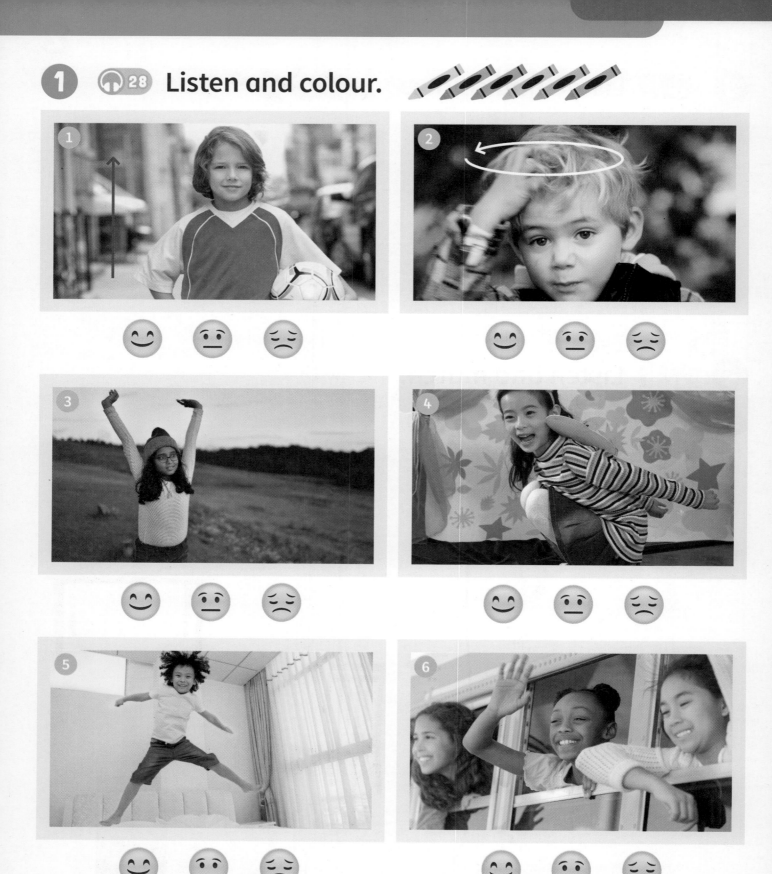

2 Look at the pictures again. Circle a face for you.

1 Look and say. Circle , or . **BIG QUESTION** How do we move?

2  Draw your favourite monster.

3 My family

1 🎧 29 Listen and colour.

1 mum

2 dad

3 sister

4 brother

5 grandpa

6 grandma

2 Look and match. Say.

1 🎧 **30** **Listen and circle.**

2 🛡 **Draw someone from your family. Circle.**

This is my …

mum   dad   brother   sister   grandpa   grandma

1 🎧 31 **Listen. Write numbers.**

mum	4
dad	☐
grandpa	☐
grandma	☐

2 🛡 **Draw your family.**

1 🎧32 Listen. Circle ☑ or ☒.

1

☑ ⊗

2

☑ ☒

3

☑ ☒

4

☑ ☒

5

☑ ☒

6

☑ ☒

1 🎧 33 **Listen and match.**

a

b

1

2

3

4

c

d

2 **Look and match.**

1

2

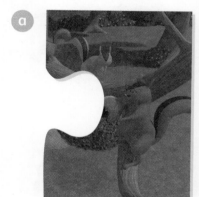
a

b

1 What's good? Draw 😊.

2 Look at the family activities. Write 1, 2 and 3.

1 🎧34 Listen and colour.

hen

dog

duck

cat

2 🛡 Draw lines to make families.

3 🎧 35 **Listen and draw.**

4 **Look and find your favourite family. Draw** 😊.

1 🎧 36 Listen and colour. Say.

1

😊 😐 😖

2

😊 😐 😖

3

😊 😐 😖

4

😊 😐 😖

5

😊 😐 😖

2 Look at the pictures again. Circle 😊, 😐 or 😖.

1 Look and say. Circle , or .

2 Complete the family and colour. Say.

 **BIG QUESTION** What's a family?

4 At the zoo

1 🎧 37 Listen and number. Say.

2 Look and draw. Say.

1

2

3      ?

1 🎧 38 **Listen and tick ✓.**

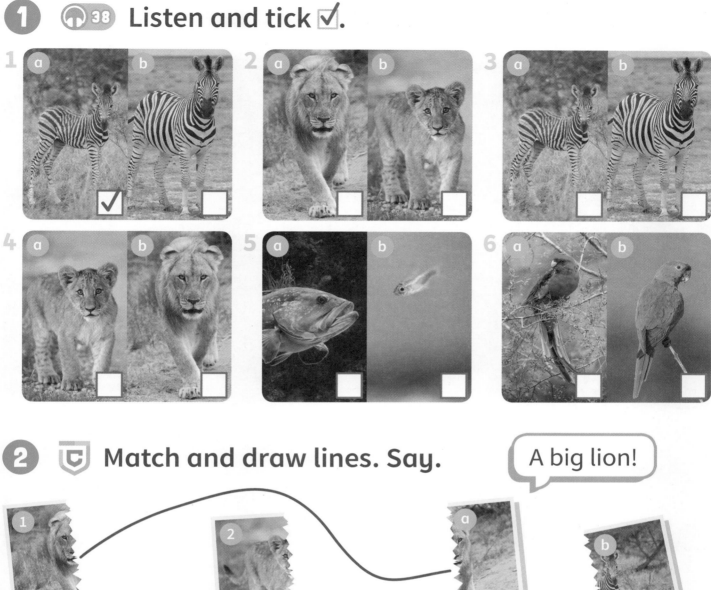

1 a ✓ b ☐

2 a ☐ b ☐

3 a ☐ b ☐

4 a ☐ b ☐

5 a ☐ b ☐

6 a ☐ b ☐

2 🛡 **Match and draw lines. Say.**

> A big lion!

1 **Look. Count and write numbers. Say.**

2	big lions
	small lions
	zebras
	small fish
	big fish
	green and orange parrots
	green and red parrots

2 big lions!

2 🎧 39 **Listen and point.**

1 🎧 40 Listen and tick ☑.

2 🎧 41 Listen and circle. Ask and answer.

What's your favourite colour?

It's red!

What's your favourite number?

It's 6!

1 🎧 42 Listen and number.

1

2 🎧 43 Listen and tick ☑.

1

2

1 What's good? Draw 😊.

2 Look at the friends. Write 1, 2 and 3.

1   Listen and colour. Say.

monkey

frog

tree

pond

grassland

2 Where do the animals live? Match and say.

The monkey lives in the tree.

3 🛡️ **Look and circle the wrong animal.**

4 🛡️ **Choose your favourite place. Draw 😊.**

1 🎧 45 **Listen and number. Say.**

a

b

c

d

e
1

2 🛡 **Draw a picture of your favourite animal.**

My favourite animal is …

1 Look and say. Circle 😊, 😐 or 😟.

2 Where do they live? Look and tick ✓.

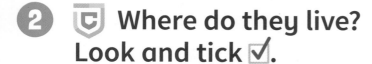 

BIG QUESTION Where can we find animals?

3 Look and think. Draw animals in the pictures.

1 Match and say.

1 cakes
2 milk
3 chocolate
4 pears
5 oranges
6 tomatoes

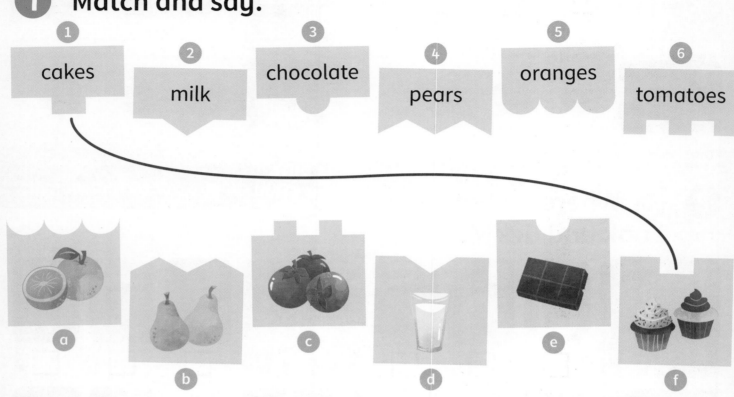

a   b   c   d   e   f

2 Look and count. Say.

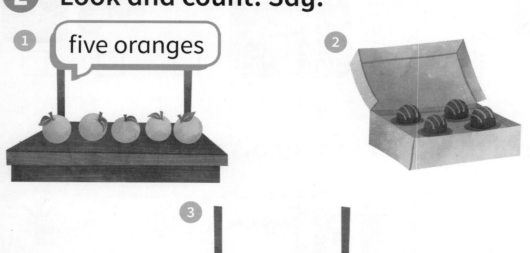

1 five oranges

2

3

4

1 🎧 46 Listen and tick ☑ or cross ☒.

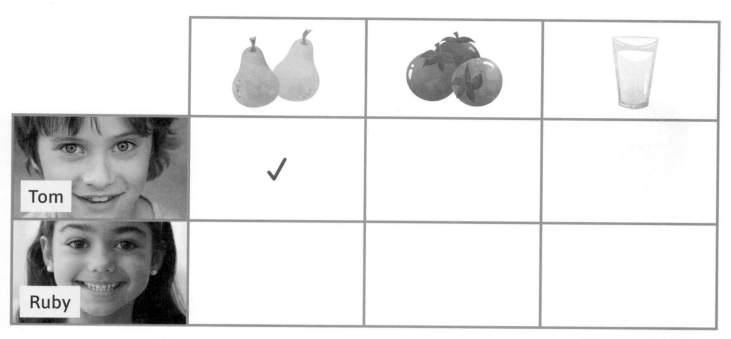

	🍐🍐	🍅🍅	🥛
Tom	✓		
Ruby			

2 🛡 Circle 😊 or 😣 for you. Say.

> I like tomatoes.

1   2   3

4   5   6

I like (oranges). I don't like (milk). (51)

1 🎧 47 **What do they like? Listen and circle.**

I like ...

1   a   b   c

I like ...

2   a   b   c

2 **Colour, trace and say.**

I like you!

1 🎧 48 Listen and write *yes* or *no*.

1

yes / no

2

yes / no

3

yes / no

4

yes / no

5

yes / no

6

yes / no

2 Look and ask.

Do you like cake?

Yes, I do.

Do you like (pink)? Yes, I do. / No, I don't. **53**

1 Follow the lines. Tick ☑ or cross ☒.

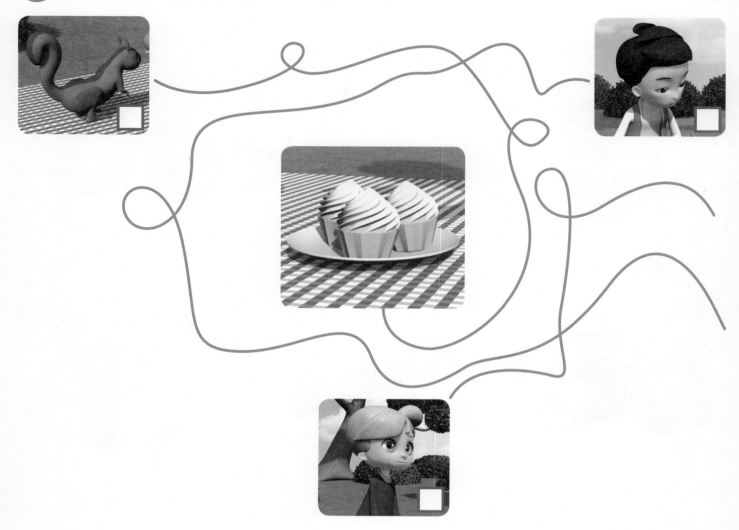

2 🛡 What's different? Look and say.

> 1 pear

1 What's good? Draw 😊.

2 Complete the picture. Draw what a good friend does.

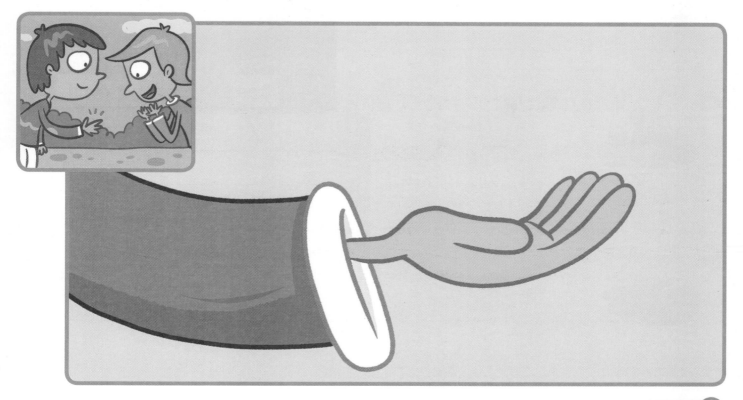

1 🛡 Which one is different? Circle.

1

a
b
c

2

a
b
c

3

a
b
c

2 🛡 Where does it come from? Trace and tick ☑.

1

apple

2

orange

3

potato

4

banana

5

pear

6

carrot

	tree	ground
1	✓	
2		
3		
4		
5		
6		

3 How many? Write.

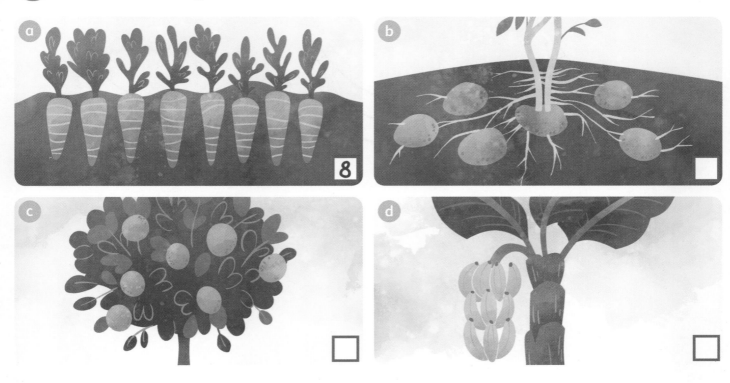

a 8

b ▢

c ▢

d ▢

4 🛡 Draw the fruit. Trace.

My ⟨fruit⟩ tree.

1 🛡 Make a 'Super Fruit'.

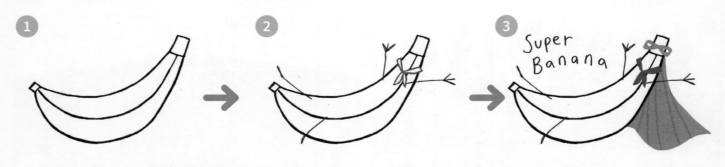

2 Show a friend.

Look – it's Super Banana!

1 Look and say. Circle , 😐 or 😟.

2 Tree or ground? Circle.

tree / ground   tree / ground   tree / ground   tree / ground

3 Choose and draw your picture.

BIG QUESTION What food do we eat?

My favourite vegetable.

1 🎧 49 Listen and number.

2 Point and say.

Bus stop

1 🎧 50 **Listen and colour.**

Ava

Bob

Mia

Nick

2 **Look at the maps. Point and say.**

There's a toy shop.

1 🎧 51 🛡 **Listen. What can you remember? Draw.**

2 **Look and write.**

park

hospital

shop

1 Look and number.

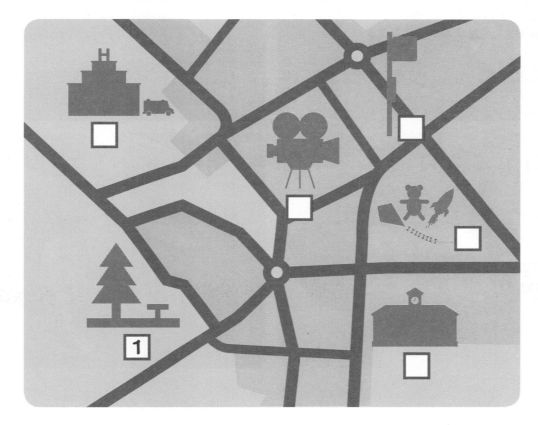

2 Look at the map. Ask and answer.

Where's the school?

It's there.

1 🎧 52 Listen and number.

a

1

b

c

d

2 🎧 53 Who says it? Listen and match.

1 There's the cinema.

2 I've got an idea!

3 Come with me.

1 What's good? Draw 😊.

2 Finish the picture. Draw what a good friend does.

1 **Where are they? Look and say.**

market

2 **Look. Write and match.**

1 **m** arket   2 ___afé   3 ___inema   4 ___ospital

3 🎧 54 **Listen and draw a line. Start at X.**

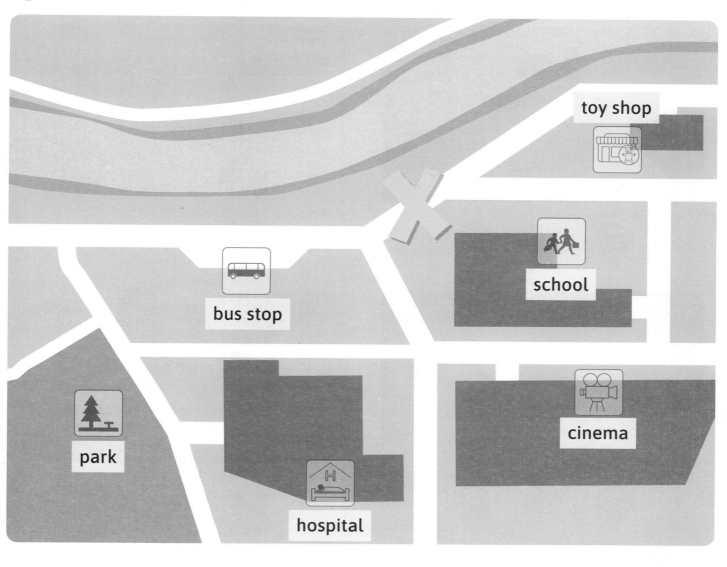

4 🛡 **Draw a place you know.**

1  **Listen and colour.**

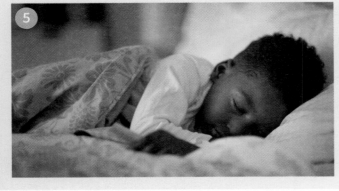

2 **Look at the pictures again. Circle a face for you.**

1 Look and say. Circle , or .

---

2 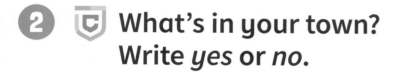 What's in your town? Write *yes* or *no*.

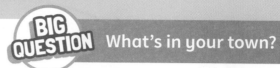 **BIG QUESTION** What's in your town?

yes / no   _____   _____   _____

---

3 Draw a picture.

Me at my favourite place.

7 Jobs

1 Match and say.

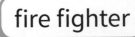
fire fighter

 1
 2
 3
 4
 5
 6

a
b
c
d
e
f

2 Look and write.

 1

 2

 3

 4

 5

 6

__t_eacher

___octor

___ardener

___et

___olice officer

___ire fighter

1 🎧 56 Listen. Write *yes* or *no*.

___yes___

2 Look at the pictures again. Say.

She's a police officer.

1 🎧57 Listen and trace.

1. hello
2. hi
3. hello
4. hi
5. hi

2 Say 'goodbye'. Write.

good___ ___ ___

7

1 🎧 58 Look. Listen and tick ☑.

1

2

3

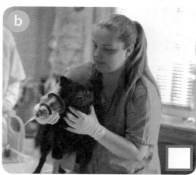

2 Point and say.

He's a police officer.

Is he/she a (fire fighter)? Yes, he/she is. No, he/she isn't.

1 Who is it? Look and match.

police officer   doctor   gardener

2 Who wears it? Write *Whisper*, *Misty* or *teacher*.

teacher

1 🛡️ **What's good? Draw 😊.**

2 🛡️ **Complete the picture.**

———————

Thank you

You are my best friend.

1 Write the first letters.

___armer   ___entist   ___hop
                                                ___ssistant

2 Circle the correct words.

1 He is inside / outside.   **2** She is inside / outside.

3 **Where are they? Look and say.**

He is outside.

4 Trace and colour.

1 Make a job picture.

My job picture

2 Trace the title.

1 Look and say. Circle , 😐 or 😔.

2 Inside or outside? Circle.

  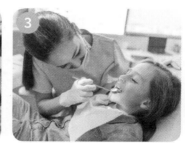 

inside / outside   inside / outside   inside / outside   inside / outside

3 Draw your favourite job.

 BIG QUESTION What's a job?

My favourite job

1 Find the words.

n	c	o	a	t	e	l	a
k	j	e	a	n	s	h	w
g	d	s	c	a	r	f	m
s	w	e	a	t	e	r	f
j	t	g	l	o	v	e	s
t	s	h	i	r	t	b	i
q	b	o	o	t	s	u	v
s	o	c	r	p	h	a	t

2 Look at pictures 1–8. Say.

sweater

1 🎧 **59** **Listen and draw.**

2 🛡 **Circle your clothes. Draw and say.**

I'm wearing ...

1 🎧 60 **What clothes do you need? Listen and circle.**

2 🛡 **Look at the picture. Tick ☑ the clothes you need.**

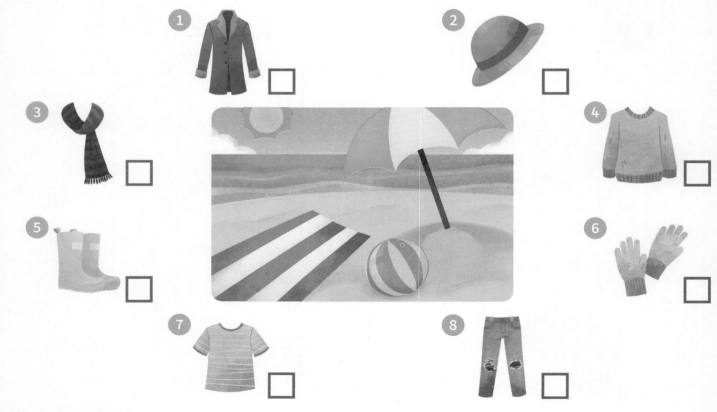

1 ☐
2 ☐
3 ☐
4 ☐
5 ☐
6 ☐
7 ☐
8 ☐

1 🎧 61 Listen. Write *yes* or *no*.

1

2

3

yes

4

5

6

2 Look at the pictures. Point and ask.

Is he wearing a scarf?

No, he isn't.

1 What's she wearing? Colour and say.

2 🎧62 Who says it? Listen and tick ☑.

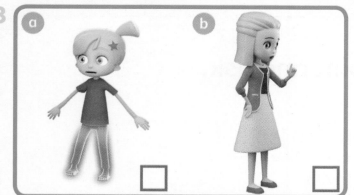

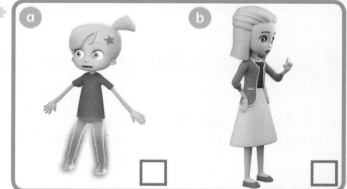

1 What's good? Draw 😊.

2 Trace the answer.

1 Complete the words. Match.

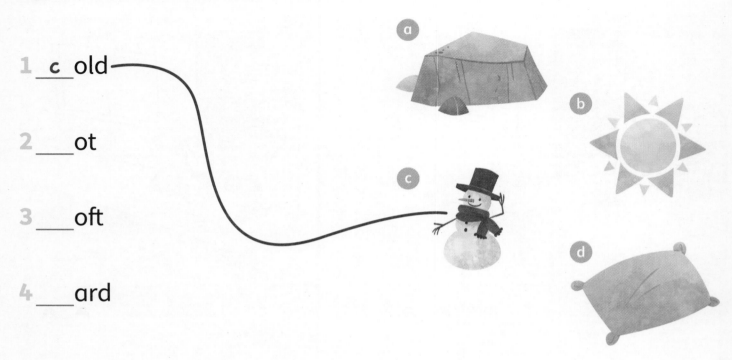

1 **_c_ old**

2 **___ ot**

3 **___ oft**

4 **___ ard**

a

b

c

d

2 Write soft or hard.

1   soft / hard

2   soft / hard

3   soft / hard

4   soft / hard

5   soft / hard

6   soft / hard

3 🛡 **Complete the words. Draw lines and match.**

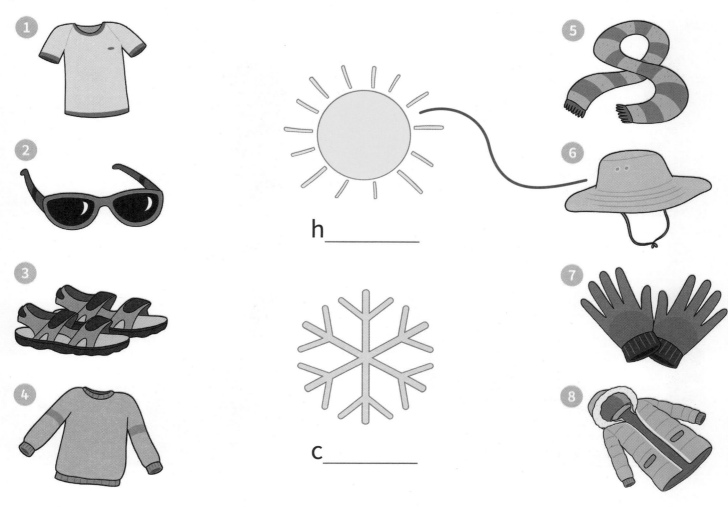

h_____

c_____

4 🛡 **Complete the picture. Trace.**

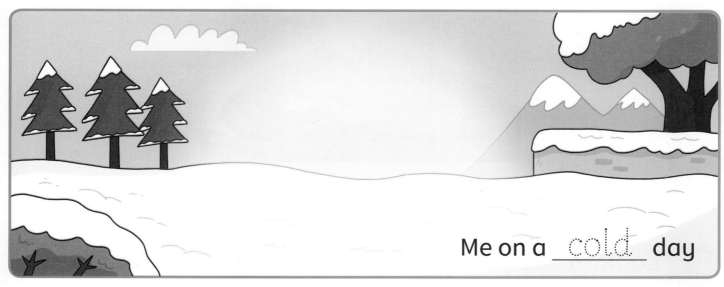

Me on a _cold_ day

1 🎧 63 Listen and colour.

2 Look at the pictures again. Circle a face for you.

8

1 Look and say. Circle .

1
2
3
4

2 Hard or soft? Circle.

1
2
3
4

hard / soft   hard / soft   hard / soft   hard / soft

3 Finish the picture.

 What clothes do we need?

My favourite T-shirt.

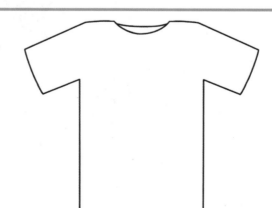

9 My hobbies

1 Circle the hobby.

1 read / swim   2 paint / dance   3 run / play football

2 Look at the pictures. Write the words.

| read | swim | dance | paint a picture | play football | run |

1 _____   2 _____   3 _____

1 Draw lines.

1. I'm playing football.

2. I'm running.

3. I'm reading.

4. I'm dancing.

5. I'm swimming.

6. I'm painting a picture.

2 Draw yourself and write.

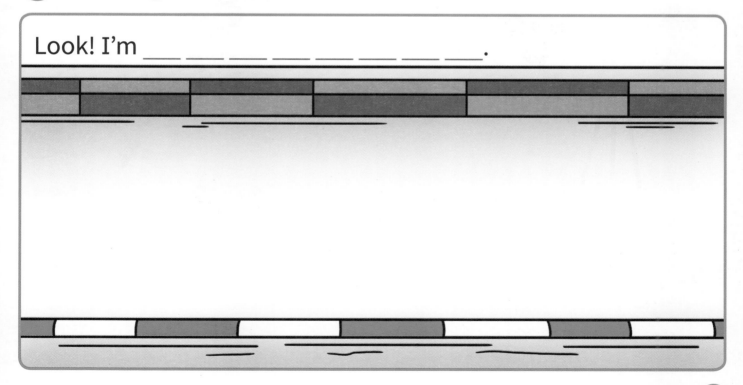

Look! I'm ___ ___ ___ ___ ___ ___ ___ .

1 🎧 64 Listen and number 1–6.

a [1]

b ☐

c ☐

d ☐

e ☐

f ☐

2 Trace.

Play today.   I'm having fun.

9

1 🎧 65 Listen. Write *yes* or *no*.

_____yes_____

_____

_____

_____

2 Look at the photos. Write.

Are you _____ _____?

Yes, I am.

Are _____ dancing?

_____, I'm _____.

1 🎧 66 Listen and number.

2 🎧 67 Who says it? Listen and tick ☑.

1 What's good? Draw 😊.

2 Write.

S _ _ _ _ _

1 Colour the bars.

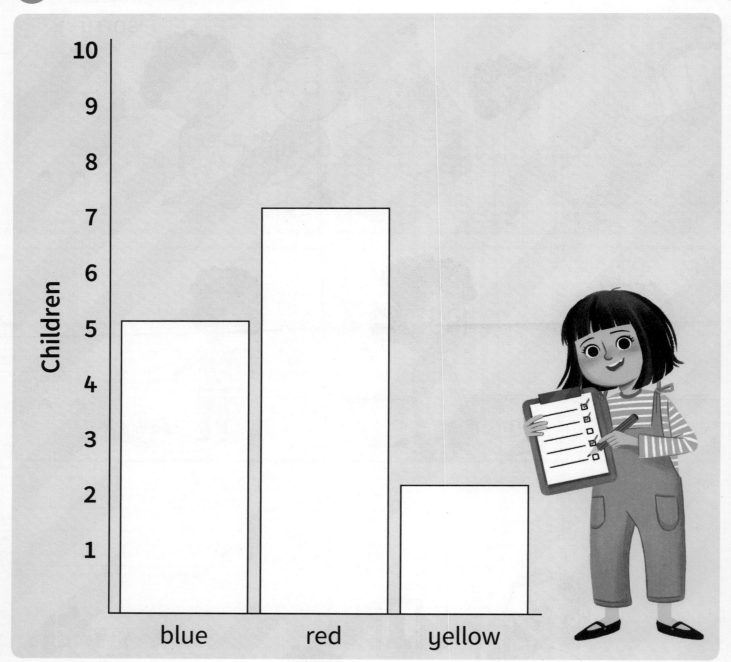

2 🛡 Count. Complete the sentences.

1 _____ children like blue.

2 _____ children like red.

3 _____ children like yellow.

3 Count and complete the tally chart.

Do you like ...?	
apples	
bananas	
oranges	

4 Draw the bar chart.

bananas

1   10

1 🛡 Make a guessing game.

What is he doing?

1 Look and say. Circle 😊, 😐 or 😞.

2 Match the numbers and pictures.

Dancing	₩₩‖
Reading	‖‖
Playing football	₩
Swimming	‖

3 Draw your favourite hobby. **BIG QUESTION** What are hobbies?

My favourite hobby

The alphabet

1 Trace the letters.

 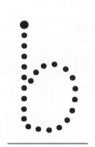  

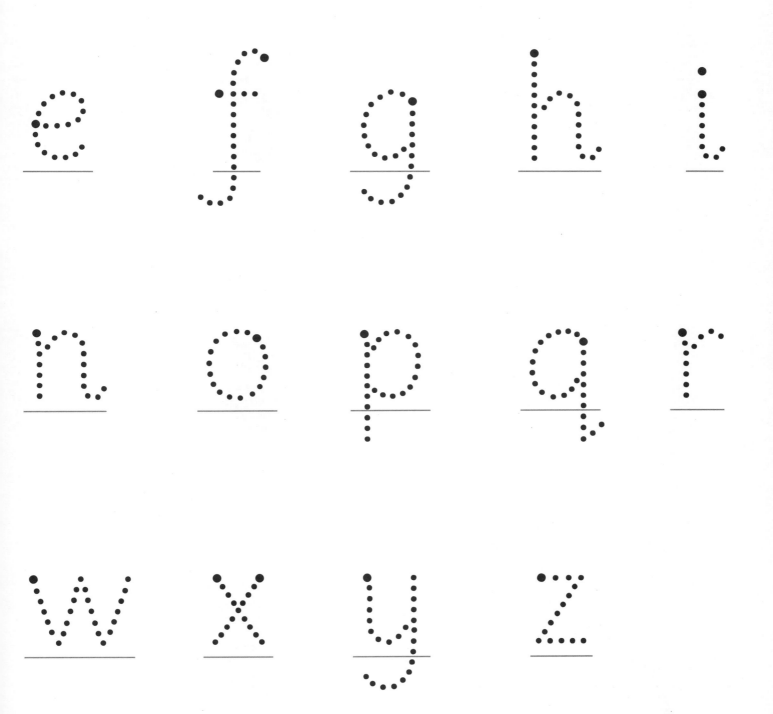

Say Hello!

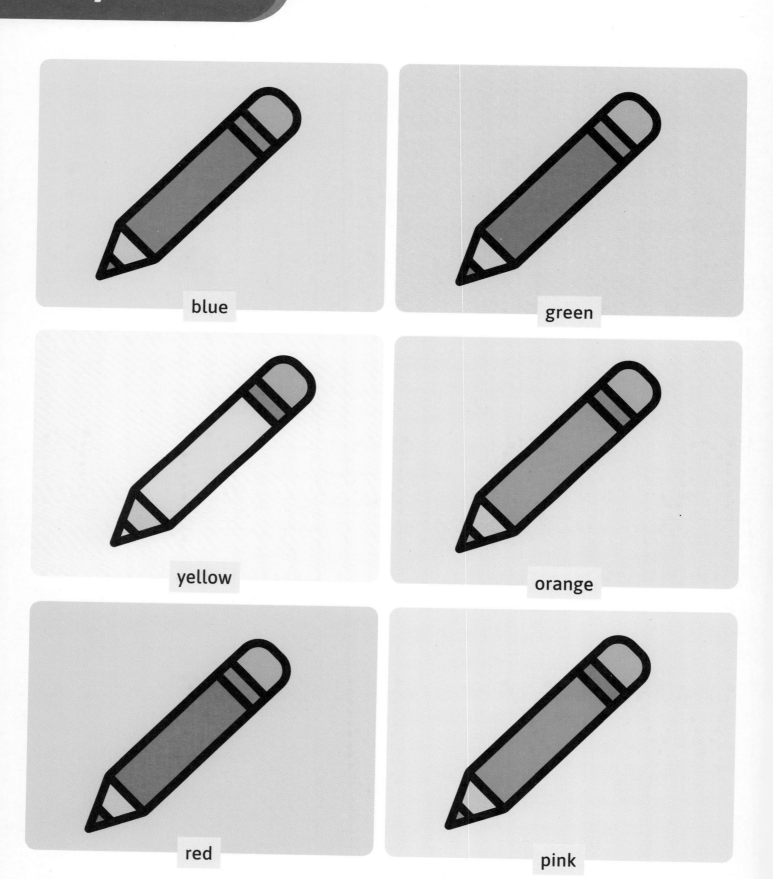

blue

green

yellow

orange

red

pink

Say Hello! (continued)

one

two

three

four

five

six

seven

eight

nine

ten

1 My classroom

window

book

table

door

pencil

chair

2 My body

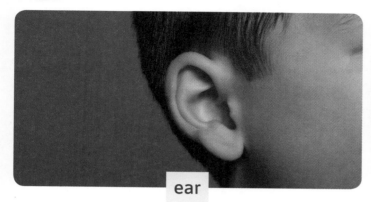
ear

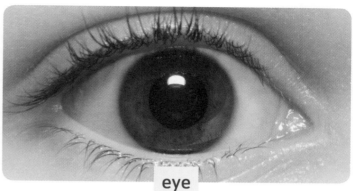
eye

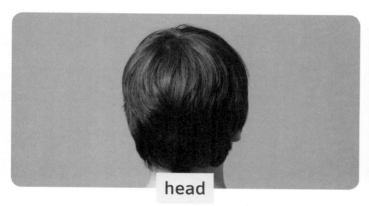
head

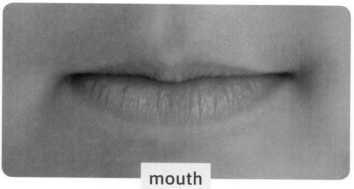
mouth

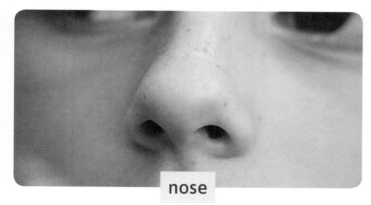
nose

arms

legs

grandma

brother

sister

grandpa

dad

mum

fish

lion

monkey

parrot

zebra

frog

5 My food

oranges

pears

tomatoes

milk

chocolate

cake

6 My town

school

toy shop

cinema

bus stop

hospital

park

teacher

police officer

doctor

vet

fire fighter

gardener

8 My clothes

____oat

____eans

____carf

____loves

____oots

____-shirt

____at

____weater

9 My hobbies

dance   paint   play football   read   run   swim

_____

_____

_____

_____

_____

_____